D0883285

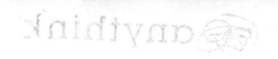

Math
in Art and Sports

Thanks to the creative team:
Senior Editor: Alice Peebles
Illustration: Dan Newman
Fact checking: Tom Jackson
Picture Research: Nic Dean
Design: Perfect Bound Ltd

Hungry Tomato®
A division of Lerner Publishing Group, Inc.
241 First Avenue North
Minneapolis, MN 55401 USA

For reading levels and more information,
look up this title at www.lernerbooks.com.

Main body text set in Panton Regular 10.5/13.

Library of Congress Cataloging-in-Publication Data

Names: Dickmann, Nancy, author.
Title: Math in art and sports / Nancy Dickmann.
Description: Minneapolis : Hungry Tomato, [2018] | Series:
The amazing world of math | Audience: Ages 8–12. |
Audience: Grades 4 to 6.
Identifiers: LCCN 2017060521 (print) | LCCN 2017056683
(ebook) | ISBN 9781541523890 (eb pdf) | ISBN
9781541500976 (lb : alk. paper)
Subjects: LCSH: Arts—Mathematics—Juvenile literature.
| Music—Mathematics—Juvenile literature. | Sports—
Mathematics—Juvenile literature. | Sports—Statistics—
Juvenile literature. | Mathematics—Juvenile literature.
Classification: LCC NX180.M33 (print) | LCC NX180.M33
D53 2018 (ebook) | DDC 700.1/51—dc23

LC record available at https://lccn.loc.gov/2017060521

Manufactured in the United States of America
1-43766-33626-2/1/2018

The Amazing World of Math

Math

in Art and Sports

Nancy Dickmann

HUNGRY TOMATO®

Minneapolis

Contents

Math
All around Us

It may seem that art and sports couldn't be further from the world of math. But if you look closely, you'll find numbers, angles, and shapes nearly everywhere.

Patterns and Angles

Did you know that the **rhythmic patterns** in music and poetry are based on numbers? Or that the **angle** of a basketball player's shot affects the ball's chances of going in the net? Even seemingly random paintings are arranged carefully, in ways that follow **geometric** patterns. Sports coaches are paying more and more attention to the patterns in **data** about their players' performance. In short, math is everywhere!

Painters such as Leonardo da Vinci used geometry to make their subjects look more realistic.

Baseball managers use **statistics** such as a player's batting average to help them make decisions.

Following the Rules

*The way that objects are arranged and framed in a painting or photo is called **composition**. Many artists use a simple rule when composing their images.*

Making Choices

Every artist—whether they're snapping a photo or painting a picture—needs to make decisions about what to show. What will be included and what will be left out? Which parts of the subject should draw the viewer's eye? Getting the composition right is the first step in creating a memorable image.

*In Claude Monet's painting, the two rock formations appear on the **vertical** lines, and the surface of the sea is on one of the **horizontal** lines.*

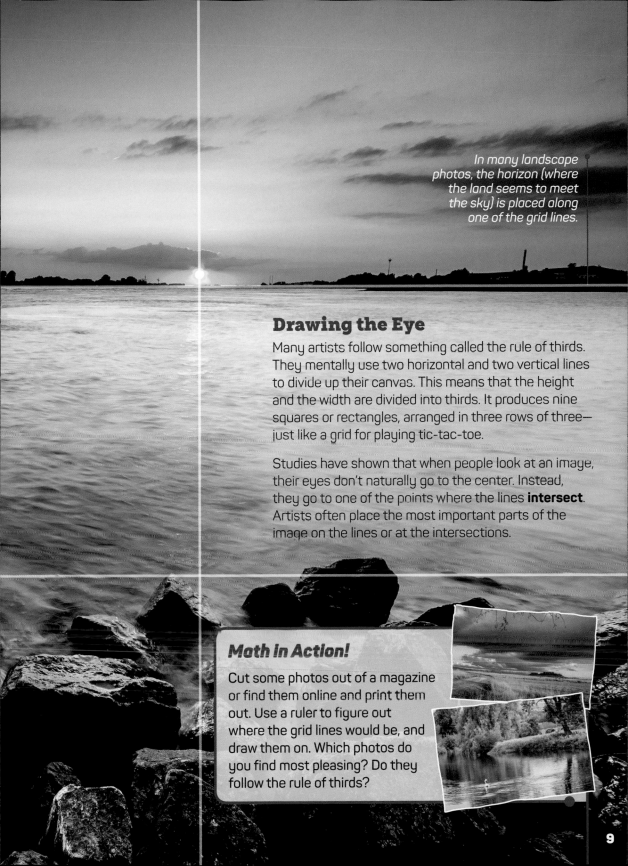

In many landscape photos, the horizon (where the land seems to meet the sky) is placed along one of the grid lines.

Drawing the Eye

Many artists follow something called the rule of thirds. They mentally use two horizontal and two vertical lines to divide up their canvas. This means that the height and the width are divided into thirds. It produces nine squares or rectangles, arranged in three rows of three—just like a grid for playing tic-tac-toe.

Studies have shown that when people look at an image, their eyes don't naturally go to the center. Instead, they go to one of the points where the lines **intersect**. Artists often place the most important parts of the image on the lines or at the intersections.

Math in Action!

Cut some photos out of a magazine or find them online and print them out. Use a ruler to figure out where the grid lines would be, and draw them on. Which photos do you find most pleasing? Do they follow the rule of thirds?

A New Dimension

The world exists in three dimensions—objects have height, width, and depth. But a painter's canvas has only two dimensions. How can they show the world realistically?

Flat Earth

For centuries, paintings and drawings showed a world that was flat, without depth. The most important figures were usually shown larger and placed at the center. Figures often seemed to float in space instead of appearing against a realistic background.

Many artists who used perspective treated the picture as an open window. The subject of the painting can be seen through it. Jesus is at the center of da Vinci's painting, The Last Supper, and the vanishing point is his right eye, which coincides with the horizon.

In paintings without **perspective**, figures were often arranged in rows.

A New Approach

During the fifteenth century, some artists learned how to create the illusion of depth in a 2D painting. In real life, the two sides of a railway track are **parallel**. But when you look at it disappearing into the distance, the lines appear to converge, or meet.

A painter could apply this effect in his paintings. He chose a point—called the **vanishing point**—on the horizon of the composition. He then sketched out a layout in which the parallel lines converged at this point. He made the objects nearer to the vanishing point look smaller, so they seemed farther away.

Math in Action!

Using a ruler, draw a horizon line across a piece of paper and mark a spot on the line—this will be your vanishing point. Draw a square somewhere else on the paper, then draw a line connecting one corner of the square to the vanishing point. Repeat for the other three corners. Now draw a smaller square behind the original one, with its corners touching the lines you just drew. Does your shape look three-dimensional?

A Matter of Degrees

Two characters in a film are having an argument. They suddenly appear to swap places. It looks like the director has just broken one of cinema's most important rules.

A scene would look boring if all the shots were taken from the same angle.

Different Angles

In any scene, a director might use several different **camera angles**. There might be a close-up of one actor's face, then a shot of another actor over the first one's shoulder. However many times the camera angle changes, the viewer needs to know where the characters are in relation to each other.

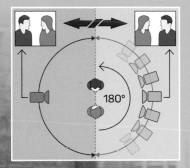

Circles and Degrees

When filming a scene, directors usually follow something called the 180-**degree** rule. A circle is divided into slices called degrees, written as °. There are 360° in a circle, so 180° make a half-circle. The rule helps the director know where to place the camera.

In a scene with two actors, a director draws an imaginary line between them. The line continues in both directions to the edge of the set. This divides the set into two halves. All the shots in the scene will be taken from the same side of the line (on the right in this diagram). If the camera moves to the other side of the line, the actors will appear to swap positions. This is very confusing for the viewer.

Math in Action!

Choose a video clip of a scene that involves two characters interacting. Draw a diagram showing the layout of the set, as seen from above. Draw a line through the characters and figure out where the cameras are placed. Does the scene follow the 180-degree rule?

Keeping Time

Music can sweep us away on a tide of emotion. But did you know that most music is based on repeated number patterns?

What is Rhythm?

In music, some notes are held for a long time and others for a shorter time. The repeating pattern of long and short notes in a piece of music forms its rhythm. Different styles of music can have very different rhythms.

Fractions in Music

When composers write down their music, they divide it into segments called **bars** or measures. Some bars may have lots of quick notes while others have just one or two long notes. However, each bar in a song lasts for the same amount of time.

Every piece of music has a **time signature**. It is written as two numbers, one over the other, like a **fraction**. The top number tells you how many beats are in a bar. The bottom number tells you which type of written note counts as one beat. So a song in 4/4 time has 4 beats in a bar, while a song in 3/4 time has just 3. Their rhythms will sound very different.

A waltz is in 3/4 time, with three beats in each bar. This means three steps for a dancer.

The time signature appears at the beginning of a piece of written music.

Musicians read musical notes and symbols in the same way that you read the math symbols in an equation.

Math in Action!

Imagine a song is written in 3/4 time and it has 30 bars. How many beats does it have in total? Imagine another song, this time written in 4/4 time. It has 80 beats in total. How many bars does it have?

15

Feeling the Beat

Like music, a lot of poetry has a regular rhythm when read aloud. It's based on number patterns too!

A poet often chooses words for the way they fit the poem's rhythm.

Stressed Out

Words are broken up into **syllables**. When we speak, we stress some syllables and leave others unstressed. For example, when saying *pizza*, we stress the first syllable but not the second. When saying *banana*, we stress the second syllable but not the first or third.

Rappers use the rhythm of their words to create a unique kind of music.

Making a Line

When you string several words together, you start to see patterns of stressed and unstressed syllables. A line of poetry is broken up into segments—units of syllable patterns called feet. The number of feet per line gives the poetry its meter, which is like the measure of music.

Poets often repeat one of these feet four or five times to make a line. For example, the famous line "The boy stood on the burning deck" is made up of four iambs. Because there are four feet in each line, it is called iambic tetrameter (*tetra* means "four" in Greek).

Here are the most common rhythms in English language poetry. The symbol ˘ means unstressed, and / means stressed.

Meter	Syllables per foot	Stresses	Example
iamb	2	˘ /	collapse
trochee	2	/ ˘	pizza
anapest	3	˘ ˘ /	but of course
dactyl	3	/ ˘ ˘	happening

Here are three lines from famous poems that illustrate different meters:

˘ / ˘ / ˘ / ˘ / ˘ /
Iambic pentameter: Was this | the face | that launched | a thou- | sand ships?

˘ ˘ / ˘ ˘ / ˘ ˘ / ˘ ˘ /
Anapestic tetrameter: And his co- | horts were glea- | ming in pur- | ple and gold

/ ˘ ˘ / ˘ ˘
Dactylic dimeter: Forward, the | Light Brigade!

Math in Action!

A poet has just finished her new poem. It has six lines, and it is written in anapestic trimeter. How many syllables does it have? (Hint: *tri* means "three" in Greek.)

Finding Angles

In sports, there are numbers on jerseys and scoreboards. But the most important math skill for a basketball player is mastering angles.

What goes up...

A basketball hoop is 10 feet (3 m) from the ground. A player throws the ball up and forward. As the ball travels across the court, **gravity** starts to pull it down to the ground. If the shooter gets the angle and the **force** just right, the ball's arc-shaped path will drop it straight through the net.

Parabolas

The ball's path is a special type of curve called a **parabola**. The two ends of the parabola are mirror images. If you throw a ball up at an angle of 70°, it will land at the same angle. When taking a shot, a player has to mentally measure his height and distance from the hoop, then work out at what angle to throw the ball.

The ball always enters the hoop at an angle. Shooting with a long, flat arc means the ball comes to the hoop at a low angle. Although the hoop is 18 inches (46 cm) across, at this angle the ball only has 9 inches (23 cm) of space to go through. Shooting from a higher angle gives the ball more space.

30° 9 inches (23 cm)

60° 12 inches (30 cm)

70° 17 inches (43 cm)

The bigger the angle, the easier it is for the ball to go through the hoop.

Math in Action!

A basketball court is rectangular, and at international size is 92 feet (28 m) long and 50 feet (15 m) wide. The perimeter is the distance around a shape. What is the perimeter of this court?

In the Hole!

In golf, you hit the ball with a club instead of throwing it at a hoop. But angles are still very important if you want to get the ball in the hole.

Obstacle Course

A golf course has slopes, water hazards, and sand traps. Before each shot, a golfer has to decide where he wants the ball to end up. It often rolls after it lands, so getting it right can be difficult.

Shooting Angles

A golf ball travels in a parabola, just like a basketball. If you hit it at a low angle, it won't fly very high, but it will travel a long way. If you hit it at a higher angle, it will fly high in the air but won't travel very far toward the hole. One reason that golfers sometimes choose a high shot is that the ball will roll less when it lands.

The clubs in a golfer's bag are all slightly different. The face of the club (the flat part that hits the ball) is set at an angle to the handle. A club with a fairly vertical face will give you a long, low shot. A club that is more angled will give you a higher, shorter shot.

It takes practice to learn the best club and stroke for each type of shot.

The angle of a golf club's face is called the loft angle.

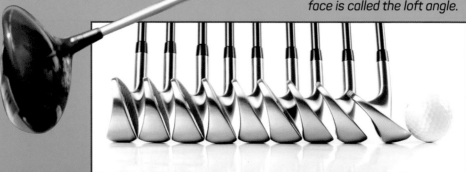

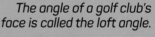

A putter is used for pushing the ball along the ground. Its face is hardly angled at all.

Math in Action!

A golfer wants to get the ball in the hole in three shots. The hole is 250 yards (229 m) away. Her first shot is 150 yards (137 m) and the second is 80 yards (73 m). How far does she need to hit the last shot?

In a Spin

A figure skater appears to glide effortlessly across the ice. She is constantly thinking about angles and rotation.

Spin Me Right Round

A skater often stays in one place on the ice while spinning rapidly. During the spin, she changes her body's position, moving from one pose to another. Some poses make her spin faster. Other poses make her slow down.

A moving object has momentum, which is a tendency to keep moving in the same direction. A spinning skater will keep spinning until a force acts to slow her down. An imaginary line from the skate blade up through her head forms the **axis** that she spins around. The farther an object's **mass** is from the axis, the more it slows down. Keeping her body tight to the axis maintains speed.

When you are spinning very fast, it takes a lot of strength to keep your body in a tight position.

Into the Air

To wow the judges, a figure skater can leap high into the air, **rotate** rapidly, and then land gracefully on the ice. It takes skill, strength, and perfect timing. To spin as fast as possible, the skater crosses her ankles and keeps her arms and hands pressed tightly against her chest. This helps her to maintain her momentum.

AXIS

Spinning in this position will be slower because the skater's leg stretches out far from the axis.

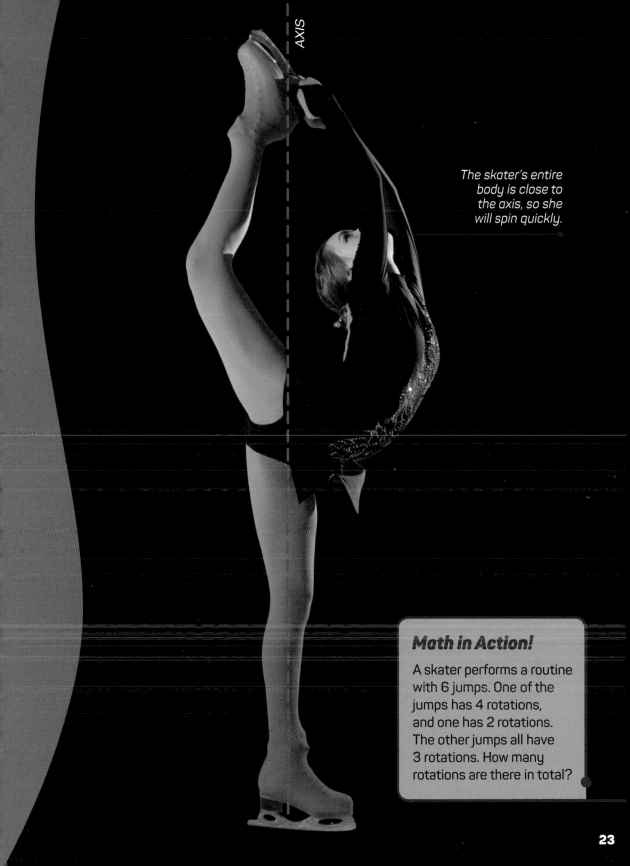

AXIS

The skater's entire body is close to the axis, so she will spin quickly.

Math in Action!

A skater performs a routine with 6 jumps. One of the jumps has 4 rotations, and one has 2 rotations. The other jumps all have 3 rotations. How many rotations are there in total?

Predicting Penalties

A penalty in a soccer match is an incredibly tense moment. The penalty kicker faces the goalkeeper one-on-one. It's a battle of wills, skills—and numbers.

A Fair Fight?

A soccer goal is 24 feet (7 m) wide and 8 feet (2 m) high. The penalty spot is only 36 feet (11 m) away, and the ball travels very fast. If the keeper waits until the ball is kicked before deciding which direction to dive, he won't be in time to stop the ball. The odds are stacked in the kicker's favor.

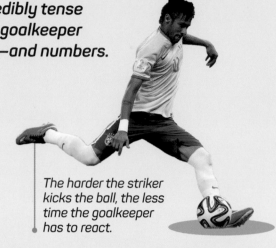

The harder the striker kicks the ball, the less time the goalkeeper has to react.

This diagram shows where penalties in World Cup shootouts have been placed. Hollow circles show saved penalties.

Knowing the Numbers

Goalkeepers try to predict which way the penalty kicker will go. They should already know which foot the penalty kicker favors and where he tends to place penalties. There may also be clues in the way the kicker runs up to the ball.

A penalty kicker may shoot more accurately in one direction. But if he always aims in the same direction, the keeper will know which way to dive. A kicker must mix things up, so his kick is not easy to predict. In the same way, a goalkeeper shouldn't always dive in the same direction. Both the goalkeeper and the kicker must consider all of these factors and make their decision.

The size of the goal means that even a 6 ½-foot-tall (2 m) goalkeeper will not be able to protect it all.

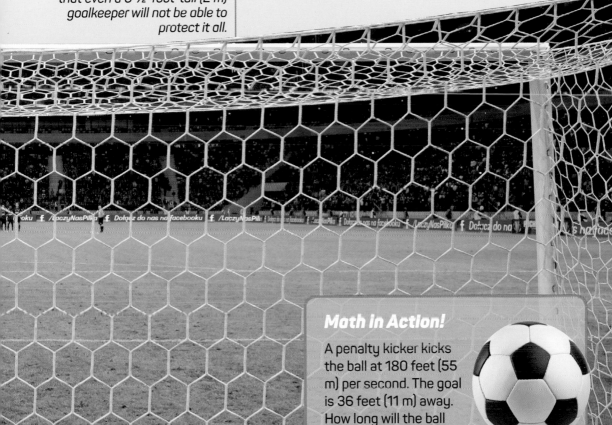

Math in Action!

A penalty kicker kicks the ball at 180 feet (55 m) per second. The goal is 36 feet (11 m) away. How long will the ball take to reach the goal?

Statistics in Sports

It's not just goalkeepers who need to use data to succeed. In all different sports, numbers are analyzed to find the best way to win.

Knowing a pitcher's average speed and pitching style can help a batter.

Crunching Numbers

In the late 1990s, baseball manager Billy Beane changed the way that teams chose players. Instead of using intuition, he looked at numbers. He figured out that players who did well in certain areas would help a team score more runs and win games. He used this strategy to choose players. Soon other managers were copying the strategy.

Super Statistics

Statistics is the branch of mathematics where you collect and analyze data, looking for patterns. In soccer, teams now keep track of how many passes a player completes, how far she runs in a match, how many successful tackles she makes, and more. The coaching staff then uses these statistics when planning training.

Technology is now providing even more numbers to analyze. Many players wear special high-tech vests. These vests have a **GPS** receiver and other devices that track the distance a player covers, their sprint speed, heart rate, and more. Afterward, the data can be downloaded onto a smartphone or computer to be analyzed.

Watching and analyzing video helps teams improve their performance.

Athletes often wear tracking vests in training. Not all sports allow them during competition.

Math in Action!

In a baseball game, a pitcher faced 30 batters. He walked 5 of them. Nine of the batters got hits and reached base safely, and 10 players grounded out. The rest struck out. What percentage of batters struck out?

Math in Action:
Answers & Tips

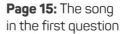

How did you do with the 10 math challenges? Here are the correct answers and some tips on how to work them out.

Page 9: When you added grids to your photos, what did you find? What parts of the composition were placed where the grid lines met? Where the compositions followed the rule of thirds, did you find them appealing?

Page 11: There is no right or wrong answer for this activity, but the more you practice, the better your perspective drawing will get. If your shape doesn't look right, check that every corner is connected to the vanishing point.

Page 13: To draw a diagram of the set, imagine that you are a bird or a drone flying above the action and looking straight down. Add the two characters first, then add any other elements such as buildings or furniture. You don't need every single detail—the position of the characters is most important. When you draw the line through them, make sure it extends to the edge of the set. Now you can figure out where the cameras are placed.

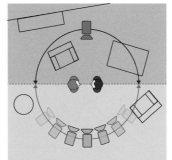

Page 15: The song in the first question has 90 beats in total. If it is written in 3/4 time, there are 3 beats in each bar. There are 30 bars, so 3 x 30 = 90.

The second song has 20 bars. If it is written in 4/4 time, there are four beats in each bar. If the song has 80 beats in total, you need to divide: 80 ÷ 4 = 20.

Page 17: The poem has 54 syllables. To figure this out, first you need to find the number of syllables in each line. The poem is written in anapestic trimeter. *Tri* means "three," so trimeter must have 3 feet in each line. An anapest has 3 syllables, so each line has 3 feet of 3 syllables each. 3 x 3 = 9, giving you 9 syllables in each line. If the poem has 6 lines, then you multiply by 6 to get the total number of syllables: 9 x 6 = 54.

Page 19: The perimeter of the basketball court is 284 feet (86 m). To find the perimeter, you add the lengths of all the sides. A rectangular basketball court has 2 sides of 92 feet (28 m) each and 2 sides of 50 feet (15 m) each. 92 + 92 + 50 + 50 = 284 (28 + 28 + 15 + 15 = 86).

You could also multiply 92 x 2 to get 184 (28 x 2 = 56), and 50 x 2 to get 100 (15 x 2 = 30). Then add the two numbers together: 184 + 100 = 284 (56 + 30 = 86).

Page 21: The golfer needs to hit the last shot 20 yd. (18 m). Add together the distances of her first two shots: 150 + 80 = 230 yd. (137 + 73 = 210 m). The total distance of the hole is 250 yd., so subtract 230 from 250 to find the answer: 250 − 230 = 20 yd. (228 − 210 = 18 m).

Page 23: The skater's routine has a total of 18 rotations. You know that there are 6 jumps in total, but you have to figure out how many rotations each one has. It might help to make a table, like this:

Jump number	How many rotations?
1	4
2	2
3	3
4	3
5	3
6	3

Because there are 6 jumps in total, you can easily see that there are 4 with 3 rotations each. Now add up all the rotations to get a total of 18.

Page 25: The ball takes ⅕ of a second (or 0.2 seconds) to reach the goal. This problem is a bit tricky because the ball travels the complete distance in less than one second. Use a calculator to divide: 180 ÷ 36 = 5. That means that in one second, the ball could travel five times as far as the distance to the goal. So it takes ⅕ of this time to travel 36 feet (11 m), the distance to the goal. ⅕ is the same as 0.2.

Page 27: To answer this question, first you need to figure out how many batters struck out. The pitcher faced 30 batters in total. You know that 5 walked, 9 got hits, and 10 grounded out, so this is a simple subtraction problem: 30 − 5 − 9 − 10 = 6.

Now you can figure out the percentage by taking the number of strikeouts (6) and finding out what percentage of 30 that is. You can do this by dividing: 6 ÷ 30 = 0.2, which is equal to 20%.

You can work this out in your head if you know that 6 x 5 = 30. This means that 6 is exactly ⅕ of 30. ⅕ is equal to ²⁄₁₀, which can be written as 0.2 or 20%.

Glossary

angle: the space between two lines that come from a central point. Angles are measured in degrees.

axis: the imaginary line through the center of an object, around which it rotates or spins

bar: in music, a segment of time containing a specific number of beats

camera angle: the location (in relation to the subject) at which a camera is placed to take a shot

composition: the way in which objects or people are arranged in a photograph, painting, or other work of art

data: facts, figures, and other information that can be used to find out about something

degree: a unit for measuring angles

dimension: a measurement of something in a particular direction, such as length, height, or width

force: a push or pull that acts on an object

fraction: a number written as one number divided by another, such as 3/4

geometric: made up of lines or shapes like those of geometry

GPS: (short for Global Positioning System) a system of satellites that communicate with receivers to show the user exactly where they are on Earth

gravity: a force that attracts all objects to one another. Gravity is the force that makes objects fall to the ground.

horizontal: going from side to side, rather than up and down

intersect: to meet or cross at a point

mass: the total amount of matter in an object or space

parabola: the curved path that an object takes when it is thrown forward into the air and then falls to the ground

parallel: being the same distance apart at every point

pattern: an arrangement of shapes, lines, or numbers that repeats over and over

perspective: a way of showing objects in two dimensions so that they seem the correct size and distance from one another

rotate: to spin around a central axis

rhythm: a strong, regular repeated pattern of sound

statistics: the science of collecting and analyzing numerical data

syllable: a unit of speech made up of a vowel sound, either with or without surrounding consonants

time signature: a pair of numbers used in music to show the rhythm of a particular piece

vanishing point: the point at which parallel lines appear to converge

vertical: going up and down, rather than from side to side

Amazing Math Facts

According to the rules set by the USGA, a golfer is allowed to carry up to 14 clubs in her bag. That's a lot of loft angles!

When composing images, some artists use a grid called a phi grid. It is like the rule of thirds, but the lines are adjusted slightly to be in line with a number called the golden ratio, which often appears in nature.

Studying statistics in baseball is such a popular activity that there is a special name for it: sabermetrics.

In basketball, bouncing the ball off the backboard can make a shot more likely to go through the net because it provides a better angle.

Sometimes film directors deliberately break the 180-degree rule. The sudden swapping of positions can make a big impact on the viewer because it is so unfamiliar and jarring.

Index

The Author

Nancy Dickmann worked in publishing for many years before becoming a full-time author. Now, with Pushkin the Three-Legged Wonder Cat as her trusty assistant (in charge of lap-sitting), she writes books on a wide range of topics, including animals, space, history, health, and explorers. The highlight of her career so far has been getting to interview a real astronaut to find out how they use the toilet in space!

Photo Credits

(abbreviations: t = top; b = bottom; c = centre; l = left; r = right)

Alamy Stock Photo: classicpaintings 8bl ; Dani Tot 18; Dziurek - Sport 1 & 24; WorldPhotos 6 & 10.

Catapult: Rafael Ribeiro 27cr.

Dan Newman: 11tr &br, 13, 19br, 28b.

Getty Images: Ross Land 27cl.

Shutterstock: AGIF 24tr; Blend Images 14; Bonita R. Cheshier 31cl; Boris Ryaposov 23; Chatchai Somwat 21 & 29b; Christian Bertrand 16; Daniel Fung 14bl & 28tr; Daxiao Productions 20tl; Dmitry Morgan 22tr & bl; Doucefleur 31tr; Eastimages 20b; ESB Professional 25tl; Eugene Onischenko 7 & 29cr; Grace Alive 9br; Grand Warszawski 12; Ingrid Curry 9br & 28c; jgolby 13br; khunkorn 31tl; Kzenon 4 & 21tr; Lightspring 3, 19r & 30; Marco Giudice and Francesca Coati 31br; matrioshka 10bl; Palokha Tetiana 25br & 29bl; Paul Gerritsen 8; stedalle 16bl; testing 2; Vector Tradition SM 27bl; zapomicron 31cr; Zhou Eka 19cr; zsolt_uveges 26; Zzvet 14tr.